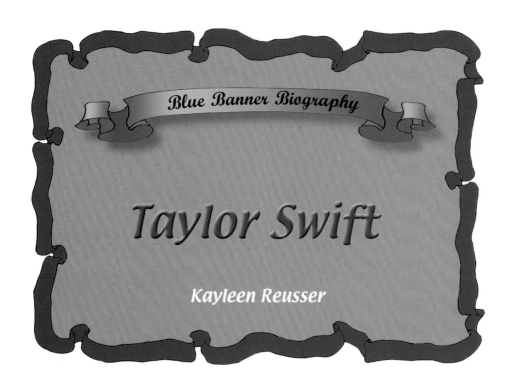

Blue Banner Biography

Taylor Swift

Kayleen Reusser

P.O. Box 196
Hockessin, Delaware 19707
Visit us on the web: www.mitchelllane.com
Comments? email us: mitchelllane@mitchelllane.com

Mitchell Lane PUBLISHERS

Printing		3	4	5	6	7	8	9

Blue Banner Biographies

Akon	Alan Jackson	Alicia Keys
Allen Iverson	Ashanti	Ashlee Simpson
Ashton Kutcher	Avril Lavigne	Bernie Mac
Beyoncé	Bow Wow	Brett Favre
Britney Spears	Carrie Underwood	Chris Brown
Chris Daughtry	Christina Aguilera	Christopher Paul Curtis
Ciara	Clay Aiken	Cole Hamels
Condoleezza Rice	Corbin Bleu	Daniel Radcliffe
David Ortiz	Derek Jeter	Eminem
Eve	Fergie (Stacy Ferguson)	50 Cent
Gwen Stefani	Ice Cube	Jamie Foxx
Joe Flacco	John Legend	Ja Rule
Jay-Z	Jennifer Lopez	Jessica Simpson
J. K. Rowling	Johnny Depp	JoJo
Justin Berfield	Justin Timberlake	Kanye West
Kate Hudson	Keith Urban	Kelly Clarkson
Kenny Chesney	Kristen Stewart	Lance Armstrong
Leona Lewis	Lil Wayne	Lindsay Lohan
Mariah Carey	Mario	Mary J. Blige
Mary-Kate and Ashley Olsen	Miguel Tejada	Missy Elliott
Nancy Pelosi	Natasha Bedingfield	Nelly
Orlando Bloom	P. Diddy	Paris Hilton
Peyton Manning	Pink	Queen Latifah
Rihanna	Ron Howard	Rudy Giuliani
Sally Field	Sean Kingston	Selena
Shakira	Shontelle Layne	Soulja Boy Tell 'Em
Taylor Swift	T.I.	Timbaland
Tim McGraw	Toby Keith	Usher
Vanessa Anne Hudgens	Zac Efron	

Library of Congress Cataloging-in-Publication Data
Reusser, Kayleen.
  Taylor Swift / by Kayleen Reusser.
    p. cm. — (Blue banner biographies)
Includes bibliographical references, discography and index.
ISBN 978-1-58415-675-8 (library bound)
1. Swift, Taylor, 1989- — Juvenile literature. 2. Women country musicians — United States — Biography — Juvenile literature. I. Title.
ML3930.S989R58 2009
782.421642092 — dc22
[B]

2008008063

ABOUT THE AUTHOR: Kayleen Reusser is a freelance writer who has published over 1,500 articles for books, newspapers, and magazines. She specializes in essay, travel, and profile articles. Reusser's stories have appeared in more than 60 publications, including *Indianapolis Monthly, Scouting,* and *Business People* magazine. This is her first book for young readers.

PUBLISHER'S NOTE: The following story has been thoroughly researched, and to the best of our knowledge represents a true story. While every possible effort has been made to ensure accuracy, the publisher will not assume liability for damages caused by inaccuracies in the data, and makes no warranty on the accuracy of the information contained herein. This story has not been authorized or endorsed by Taylor Swift.

Blue Banner Biography

Taylor Swift shows her songwriting ability and talent as a performer by singing a tune she wrote, "Our Song," at the 41st Annual Country Music Association Awards show on November 7, 2007, in Nashville, Tennessee.

The Big Night

*S*eventeen-year-old Taylor Alison Swift hurried through the Sommet Center in Nashville, Tennessee. All around the building she could see preparations for that evening's Country Music Association (CMA) Awards show. Taylor's heart pounded with excitement. She had been asked to sing for one of the biggest country music events of the year!

In the dressing room, Taylor put on makeup while chatting with Kellie Pickler. The girls had met the previous summer while traveling with Brad Paisley's tour.

Kellie, another young country music singer, was also planning to sing that night. Performing was a tradition for Horizon Award nominees—and both girls had been nominated. According to a press release posted on Taylor's web site, the Horizon Award is given each year by the Country Music Association to a new country music singer who records hit songs, is written about a lot in newspapers and magazines, and is a professional live performer.

Taylor Swift and Kellie Pickler became friends while traveling with Brad Paisley during the summer of 2007 on his Bonfires and Amplifiers Tour. At 5 feet 11 inches, Taylor is taller than most female country music artists.

Taylor wanted to win the Horizon Award. She knew that many people who won, such as Garth Brooks and Keith Urban, became country music superstars. She also knew the rest of the nominees for the 2007 Horizon Award—Jason Aldean, Rodney Atkins, and the group Little Big Town—wanted to win too. Taylor decided not to worry about it and left the dressing room to rehearse with her band.

Later, she answered questions for reporters during media interviews. Back in the dressing room, she put on a beautiful floor-length gold dress with a flared skirt. Then she joined the other country music artists in posing for photos, including one for the magazine *Country Weekly*.

Backstage again, Taylor quickly changed into the short, sleeveless black dress she would wear for her performance.

With it, she wore a headband in her long blond hair and black gloves that came up to her elbows. She also wore boots, as she often does to perform.

For her song, Taylor was raised on a platform through the floor of the stage while playing her guitar. It looked like she was blooming from a flower. Taylor wrote about the experience the next day on her blog: "I loved it, not gonna lie."

The song Taylor performed was "Our Song," which she had written in the ninth grade. The performance went well. In the dressing room again, she changed back into her gold dress and heels and sat down with the audience to watch the rest of the show.

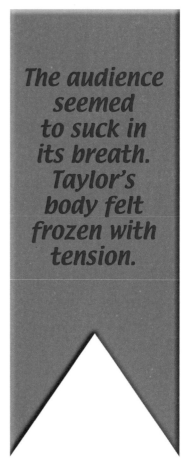

The audience seemed to suck in its breath. Taylor's body felt frozen with tension.

When Carrie Underwood walked onstage, Taylor's heart started to pound. Carrie would announce the new Horizon Award winner. Taylor grabbed Rodney Atkins' hand from across the aisle and held it for good luck.

Carrie called out each nominee's name. Then she said, "And the award goes to . . ."

The audience seemed to suck in its breath. Taylor's body felt frozen with tension.

Carrie smiled. "Taylor Swift!"

Taylor covered her face with her hands. She hugged her mother and Rodney, then walked quickly to the stage.

In 2007, Taylor received the Horizon Award, given each year at the Country Music Association Awards show. The Horizon is considered a prestigious award because it recognizes promising new singers. Winning the award can boost a singer's career.

Holding the Horizon statue, Taylor saw her parents crying from their seats. She wrote two days later that she knew her family and friends watching on TV were happy for her.

"I can't believe this is real!" Taylor told the audience. "I want to thank God and my parents for moving to Nashville so I could do this." She continued thanking people, including the fans of country music for buying her records.

At the end of her short speech, Taylor surprised everyone by saying, "This is the highlight of my senior year!"

The crowd roared with laughter.

That night, November 7, 2007, it was hard to remember that Taylor Swift was still in high school. After watching her play her guitar on stage, one might think she had been singing for years. The truth was, she had been performing for audiences since childhood.

Taylor, or the Country Teen Queen, as *People Weekly* called her, was thrilled to win the Horizon Award. But that was not all she wanted to do. She wanted to become a country music star. Winning the Horizon Award was a step in the right direction.

At the end of her short speech, Taylor surprised everyone by saying, "This is the highlight of my senior year!"

In 2008, country music newcomer Taylor Swift was nominated for a Grammy Award for Best New Artist. Amy Winehouse won the award.

The Dream

*I*n 1998, when Taylor Swift was eight years old and living in Wyomissing, Pennsylvania, she heard LeAnn Rimes sing "Blue" on the radio. Rimes was a teenager when her song became a hit.

Taylor loved "Blue" and wanted to be a singer like Rimes. In school, when Taylor performed a song in choir, she sang like Rimes. The problem was, people in Wyomissing didn't speak like LeAnn Rimes, who is from Mississippi. And country music was not as popular in Pennsylvania as it was in the South.

Taylor didn't let her accent stop her. She wanted to be a professional singer like her grandmother, who sang opera. Instead of opera, though, Taylor wanted to sing country music like Shania Twain, Faith Hill, and the Dixie Chicks.

At home when she wasn't helping on her family's Christmas tree farm or relaxing with them on their boat,

Taylor did everything she could to become a professional country music singer. By age ten she was singing regularly at karaoke contests, festivals, and fairs.

Taylor knew she wouldn't get discovered by a talent agent at a county fair. She sang there because she wanted to prepare for Nashville. "I wanted to get better, so that when I did go to Nashville, I'd be a seasoned performer," she wrote on her web site. "There's no use walking into a record label to 'get your big break' if you're not practiced enough to get it."

"There's no use walking into a record label to 'get your big break' if you're not practiced enough to get it."

When she was younger, Taylor had felt scared standing in front of large groups of people. But as she continued performing, she grew accustomed to it. "I used to get nervous when I was a little kid," she wrote, "but that wears away with time. . . . It just comes with going out and playing shows over and over until you don't get even a slight bit nervous anymore."

Taylor's love for language helped her win a national poetry contest in the fourth grade. When she was eleven, she sang the national anthem in front of thousands of people at a Philadelphia 76ers basketball game. But it wasn't enough to make her famous.

Most country music is recorded in Nashville, so Taylor's family traveled there in 2001. Taylor recorded herself singing Dixie Chicks tunes, and she and her mother handed out CDs

Taylor gets inspiration for her songs from everyday life. "I look around at what is happening to me and my friends. The more drama, the better," she says.

of it to record company officials. Taylor told Ellen DeGeneres years later that she had walked into every music company in the city, handed them a CD, and said, "Hi, I'm Taylor. I'm eleven and want a record deal. Call me."

None of the record companies called Taylor after she returned home, but she didn't give up. Instead, she tried to think of what she could do to be different from other singers. She told CMT (Country Music Television) that she thought of songwriting. If she could write her own music, she would stand out in a crowd.

Taylor learned how to play a twelve-string guitar. When she knew three chords, she wrote a song.

One of her early tunes, "The Outside," described what it felt like to be left out. Taylor's web site biography tells how she had often felt lonely.

> *She was spending every moment writing songs on guitar or piano. "I'd practice for four hours a night until my fingers were bleeding."*

Taylor wrote another song, then another. She played her music for anyone who would listen. Soon, she was spending every moment writing songs on guitar or piano. "I'd practice for four hours a night until my fingers were bleeding," she told Ellen.

Taylor and her family again traveled to Nashville. This time Taylor handed out CDs of her singing her own songs. Two major music companies liked what they heard and offered Taylor songwriting jobs. She first signed with RCA, then switched to Sony/ATV Music Publishing.

The songwriting job was a challenge. "I wrote every day after school, and that knocked out any extracurricular activities I might have done otherwise," she later wrote.

But Taylor wanted to do more than write songs. She also wanted to sing and perform her music on stage. She knew that to get the chance she needed, she would have to live in Nashville.

Connected in
Nashville

*T*aylor's parents—Scott, a financial adviser, and Andrea, a homemaker—knew how hard their daughter had worked to become a country music singer. Taylor had given up attending slumber parties as a young girl to attend festivals and other events where she could sing. She had also earned good grades at school while writing for a major record company.

Her younger brother, Austin, excelled at sports and had no interest in music. Still, he also supported Taylor's desire to succeed in music.

When Taylor was thirteen, the Swift family moved to Hendersonville, Tennessee, outside of Nashville. At Hendersonville High School, Taylor still was a good student, but she studied her friends as well as her books. She told *People Weekly*, "There was always some drama I could write songs about, like my friend getting broken up with and bawling her eyes out or a guy being completely immature."

Taylor attends the 42nd Annual Academy of Country Music
Awards show on May 15, 2007, in Las Vegas with her mother,
Andrea Swift. Taylor's mother tours with her while Taylor's father,
Scott, and brother, Austin, live at the family's home in Nashville.

Many singers move to Nashville, hoping to get a record deal. Taylor knew the competition would be stiff, but she didn't give up. As often as she could, she found someplace to sing her tunes.

One day she was playing her guitar and singing at the Bluebird Cafe—a relaxed restaurant where talented singers often gather to play and be heard. Someone in the audience asked to speak with her.

Scott Borchetta had listened to Taylor and liked what he heard. He planned to start his own record company. Taylor told Ellen that he had asked her to join his team of musicians once he was ready. She agreed. In fall of 2005, she signed on as a singer with Borchetta's new company, Big Machine Records. She was fifteen years old.

Taylor wanted to write all the songs for her first album. "As a songwriter, it's a lot easier to show people who you really are when you're singing songs that come directly from your thoughts," she wrote. "It's so cool to look down into a crowd of people and see them singing the lyrics to songs you wrote. That's an awesome feeling."

> "It's so cool to look down into a crowd of people and see them singing the lyrics to songs you wrote. That's an awesome feeling."

Taylor ended up writing three of the songs on the album by herself. She worked with Liz Rose, another songwriter, on the others. In an interview with Dale Kawashima, Taylor said she loved writing with Liz. "When we write, I usually come in with a melody and some lyric content and then we'll work on creating the rest of the song," she said. "Liz is a really good song editor."

Together, they wrote Taylor's first single, "Tim McGraw."

Some people thought "Tim McGraw" was about the country music singer by that name. But Taylor told Kawashima the song was really about a Tim McGraw song she and her boyfriend had liked. "I had a boyfriend and we had broken up. After the break-up, I wanted him to be reminded of me [whenever he heard the song]." After its release in the summer of 2006, "Tim McGraw" rose to number 6 on the Billboard country radio charts.

> "I had a boyfriend and we had broken up. After the break-up, I wanted him to be reminded of me."

Making it into the Top 10 was an amazing accomplishment for a new singer and songwriter. Taylor spent the summer traveling the country, meeting radio personalities, and playing "Tim McGraw" for anybody who would listen.

On February 24, 2007, Taylor's record company released another song she wrote. "Teardrops on My Guitar" was about a boy Taylor had liked, but who liked another girl and always told Taylor about how much he liked the other girl. According to *Country Weekly*, when "Teardrops on My Guitar" landed at the number 2 spot on Billboard's charts, it became the biggest hit by a teenager since LeAnn Rimes' "One Way Ticket (Because I Can)" in 1996.

While Taylor was thrilled with the success of her first two songs, she still didn't have a number one song on the music charts. Her next release would be one she said she had written for a ninth-grade talent show. Would it become her first number one hit?

Taylor Swift sings the national anthem at a game between the Los Angeles Dodgers and the Colorado Rockies on April 9, 2007. She had come a long way since playing a similar gig at a Philadelphia 76ers basketball game when she was eleven.

Awards and Accolades

*D*uring 2007, Taylor and her band opened concerts for Rascal Flatts, Kenny Chesney, George Strait, Brad Paisley, and Tim McGraw and Faith Hill. They played for over one million people. Everything was going well for Taylor.

In August 2007, Big Machine Records released Taylor's third single to radio stations. Taylor had written and sung "Our Song" for a talent contest when she was a freshman in high school. She knew "Our Song" was special when months after the contest, people came up to her and sang it. "I thought, 'You know what? They've only heard this once, so there must be something to this song,' " she told *Country Weekly*.

"Our Song," "Tim McGraw," and "Teardrops on My Guitar" were all recorded on the album *Taylor Swift*. As the three songs were played more and more often by radio stations, the album steadily climbed the Billboard chart. On

Taylor Swift has driven herself to success with hard work, determination, and a love for music and people.

July 25, 2007, it became the number one country album in America! Taylor was thrilled. But that was just one of many good things to happen to her career that year.

In November a limited Deluxe Edition CD/DVD of *Taylor Swift* and a Christmas album *(Sounds of the Season: The Taylor Swift Holiday Collection)* were released.

Taylor celebrated her eighteenth birthday on December 13, 2007, at a big party with family and friends. She had a lot to celebrate. "Our Song" had reached the number one position on the Billboard Hot Country Songs chart.

"Our Song" did more than hit the number one position. It also helped Taylor become a part of country music history. According to a press release on her web site, she became the youngest person to write and sing a number one country song on her own.

She was also one of only three women country artists since 2000 to have three straight Top 10 songs from a first album. Gretchen Wilson and Carrie Underwood were the other two singers to accomplish that.

"Our Song" became one of the Top 10 most-added songs on the Facebook chart. Taylor was the only country music artist on the chart. Within a few weeks, her music had been played more than 35 million times over her MySpace page.

> *Her music had been played more than 35 million times over her MySpace page.*

Perhaps most remarkable of all was when sales for the album *Taylor Swift* passed two million copies. It was now a multiplatinum album! (*Platinum* is the label an album receives when it sells one million records.) Taylor became the first female solo artist in country music history to write or cowrite all the songs on a platinum-selling debut CD. By the end of 2007, *Taylor Swift* had spent more time at the top of the country sales chart than any other country music album that year.

Taylor also earned a number of honors and awards during this time, including the 2007 CMT Music Award for Breakthrough Video for "Tim McGraw." She became the youngest artist to ever win the Songwriter/Artist of the Year award from the Nashville Songwriters Association International. Two of her videos, "Our Song" and "Teardrops on My Guitar," made the Top 50 of 2007 for the Great American Country cable TV channel. The editors of *Justine,* a magazine for teen girls, chose Taylor to be on the cover of the December 2007/January 2008 issue.

Perhaps most rewarding of all, she was nominated for a Grammy Award for Best New Artist. She was also named Country Music's Hottest Female Artist by AOL Music.

Taylor was nominated for Best New Female Artist by the Academy of Country Music. When iTunes released its Best of 2007 Editor's Choice list, Taylor was named the Best New Artist.

Taylor ended the year by participating in the annual ABC special *Dick Clark's New Year's Rockin' Eve 2008* on December 31. Clark had hosted the show since the 1970s. It has become a favorite tradition for millions of viewers to watch the show and welcome in the New Year.

Being asked to perform on Dick Clark's show is like being on an awards show. Clark asks only the best singers in America to perform. Multiplatinum American Music Award–winning artist Fergie hosted and sang during the West Coast part of the show in Hollywood. Ryan Seacrest from *American Idol* helped Clark host the New York portion. Besides Taylor, the Plain White T's, Sean Kingston, Natasha Beddingfield, will.i.am, OneRepublic, Carrie Underwood, Miley Cyrus, and the Jonas Brothers all performed musical hits for the show.

> When iTunes released its Best of 2007 Editor's Choice list, Taylor was named the Best New Artist.

It may seem as though all her dreams of being a country music star have come true. But Taylor is not just a singer searching for fame and glory. She also cares about people, especially children and teens. She makes time in her busy life to help them.

Thinking of
Others

*T*aylor Swift has worked hard to be a great singer and musician. She spends much time on the road, traveling to concerts, writing music, and attending special events.

But Taylor has not let success spoil her attitude. "I think with something like this, it's all about the people you keep around you," she told a reporter from Great American Country TV. "If you keep people around you who knew you when you were a little kid, they'll realize when you're changing. You have to realize you're no different than anyone else."

Taylor cares about the people she meets and has helped them, many times as a volunteer. She began volunteering when she was twelve years old. "Both of my grandparents had cancer, so I spent every day for probably six months in the hospital after school," she said. "I took my guitar to the hospital after school and played music for them and anybody in the cancer ward that wanted to hear music."

Taylor has also volunteered with a group of people in Tennessee who teach parents and middle school students about the dangers of surfing the Internet. "Chatting with friends and surfing the Internet is cool," Taylor says. "But it's important to stay safe. Be smart about keeping your identity private online."

In December 2007, Taylor helped judge the Holiday Holla competition at the Mall of America in Minnesota. Teenagers were encouraged to write new words to traditional Christmas songs about the importance of driving safely. The teens performed their songs before the judges, who then picked the best one. After the judging, Taylor gave a concert for the crowd.

When Taylor's record company gave her a pink extended-cab Chevy pickup truck for her eighteenth birthday, Taylor donated it to Victory Junction Gang, a camp for kids with health needs. The camp will use the truck to ferry campers to and from the airport.

Another way Taylor helps people is by offering advice about how to get into the music business. One thing she always tells people is to "be yourself."

> *One thing she always tells people is to "be yourself." "Forget about what's 'in.' Being different is what's really 'in.'"*

"Forget about what's 'in.' Being different is what's really 'in,' " she told *Country Weekly*.

Taylor's busy schedule often keeps her on the road. Everywhere she goes, she thinks about people who come to hear her perform. This helps her make decisions. "I think

When performing at MTV's TRL Studios in New York City on February 27, 2008, Taylor played her sparkly guitar, a fan favorite. It was the inspiration for the crystal guitar made for the Taylor Swift doll, manufactured by JAKKS.

about the ten-year-old girl I saw at my concert in the front row," she wrote on her web site. "I think about her mom. I think about how they bought my CD, thinking that I'm a good role model. Then I think about how they would feel if I did something to let them down. I can't imagine a greater pain than letting one of those mothers down. I honestly can't."

Taylor thinks part of being a role model is wearing the right clothes. "I'm not really into showing a lot of skin," she told *Country Weekly*. "I'd rather have the girls in the crowd thinking, 'That outfit's really cute,' than having the guys thinking, 'Man, that's hot.' "

Girls who attend Taylor's concerts like her choices of dresses and boots. Her fans often wear similar clothes to the concerts.

This is fine with Taylor. Her clothes are comfortable and make her feel good about herself. "If you walk into a room looking like you're confident about what you're wearing, you'd be surprised how far that will go," she said.

With all her traveling, Taylor made the choice to complete her last two years of high school through homeschooling. When she is asked if she ever feels like she missed the normal life of a teenager, she always says no.

"There are times when everybody in the arena is just screaming," she said. "And I'm thinking, 'This is exactly why I wanted to do this.' "

> "There are times when everybody in the arena is just screaming," she said. "And I'm thinking, 'This is exactly why I wanted to do this.' "

Taylor may have been thinking of those moments when she wrote these words to her song "A Place in This World": "Maybe I'm just a girl on a mission, but I'm ready to fly."

Taylor Swift is flying high in her goal to be a country music star. How high she will go is anyone's guess.

1989 Taylor Alison Swift is born on December 13.

2000 She begins singing at karaoke festivals.

2001 Taylor sings at a Philly 76ers NBA game; she wins a national poetry contest; she and her mother hand out CDs of Taylor's singing to music companies in Nashville.

2003 Taylor's family moves to Nashville.

2004 Taylor lands an artist development deal with BMI and RCA Records.

2005 She lands a publishing deal with Sony/ATV Music Publishing. In the fall, she signs with Big Machine Records.

2006 Taylor is featured in a behind-the-scenes series from GAC (Great American Country) *Short Cuts* documentary. Her first music video debuts on GAC. Her debut album *Taylor Swift* is released and is promoted on the channel's web site.

2007 Taylor wins the CMA's Horizon Music Award. *Taylor Swift* goes gold, then double platinum. "Our Song" is a number one hit; three of Taylor's singles rank among country radio's Top 10. Her holiday album is released. She is nominated for a Grammy Award, and tops the Country Album Sales chart longer than any other artist this year. "Teardrops on My Guitar" takes over the number one position on GAC's fan-voted Top 20 Countdown and is lauded by iTunes as its number one selling country song for the year. Her MySpace streams surpass 31 million, averaging 100,000 per day. She is nominated for three Academy of Country Music Awards: Top Female Vocalist, Top New Female Vocalist, and Album of the Year (*Taylor Swift*).

2008 Taylor makes her debut as a video director with her new video "I'm Only Me When I'm With You." JAKKS plans to launch a line of Taylor Swift fashion dolls and accessories, including Swift's signature crystal guitar. She is featured on the cover of *Rolling Stone* magazine's Best of Rock 2008 issue. She releases her second album, *Fearless*, in November. In April, her MySpace streams pass 45 million. She wins Best New Female Vocalist by the Academy of Country Music.

2009 Taylor performs a duet of her single "Fifteen" with pal Miley Cyrus at the 51st Annual Grammy Awards. By the middle of March, her album *Fearless* was still holding the number one spot on the charts.

ACHIEVEMENTS

Discography
Albums
2008   *Fearless*
2007   *Limited Deluxe Edition CD/DVD of Taylor Swift*
2006   *Sounds of the Season: The Taylor Swift Holiday Collection*
        Taylor Swift

Singles
2009   "Fearless"
2008   "Love Story"
        "Picture to Burn"
        "Should've Said No"
2007   "Our Song"
        "Teardrops on My Guitar"
2006   "Tim McGraw"

Awards
2008   Named Best New Female Vocalist by the Academy of Country
        Music
        Wins two CMT Awards: Video of the Year and Female Video of
        the Year for "Our Song"
        Nominated for Favorite Female Country Artist at American
        Music Awards
2007   Wins Country Music Association's Horizon Award
        Wins CMT Breakthrough Video of the Year Award for "Tim
        McGraw"
        Wins Songwriter Achievement Award for her debut single "Tim
        McGraw"
        Wins the Nashville Songwriters Association International
        Songwriter / Artist of the Year Award (she is the youngest
        artist ever to win the award)
        Named Country Music's Hottest Female by AOL Music
        Named Best New Artist on iTunes Best of 2007 Editor's
        Choice List
        Nominated for a Grammy Award for Best New Artist
        Nominated for Best New Female Vocalist by the Academy of
        Country Music

Books

If you enjoyed this biography of Taylor Swift, you might also enjoy these other country music Blue Banner Biographies from Mitchell Lane Publishers:

Adams, Michelle Medlock. *Kenny Chesney*. Hockessin, Delaware: Mitchell Lane Publishers, 2007.

Adams, Michelle Medlock. *Tim McGraw*. Hockessin, Delaware: Mitchell Lane Publishers, 2007.

Leavitt, Amie Jane. *Keith Urban*. Hockessin, Delaware: Mitchell Lane Publishers, 2008.

Torres, Jennifer. *Alan Jackson*. Hockessin, Delaware: Mitchell Lane Publishers, 2007.

Tracy, Kathleen. *Carrie Underwood*. Hockessin, Delaware: Mitchell Lane Publishers, 2006.

Works Consulted

Butler, Susan. "Growing Pains." *Billboard,* May 21, 2005, Vol. 117, Issue 21, p. 14.

"CMA Awards: Big Prizes, Big Surprises." *Country Weekly,* December 3, 2007, p. 40.

"CMA Nominees: And The Winner Is?" *Country Weekly,* November 5, 2007, p. 26.

The Ellen DeGeneres Show. January 17, 2008. (VHS tape of show available.)

Finan, Eileen. "Taylor Swift Country's Teen Queen." *People Weekly,* May 21, 2007, http://find.galegroup.com/itx/start.do?prodId=GRGM>.

Finan, Eileen, and Ericka Souter. "Taylor Swift: Her Bedroom." *People Weekly, Country Special,* Fall 2007, pp. 52–53, http://find.galegroup.com/itx/start.do?prodId=GRGM.

Hasty, Katie. "Swift's Un-Swift Climb." *Billboard,* August 4, 2007, Vol. 119 Issue 31, p. 9.

Haugsted, Linda, Todd Spangler, and Tom Steinert-Threlkeld. "Taylor Swift Follows Path Rimes Forged." *Multi-Channel News,* March 19, 2007.

Jessen, Wade. "Taylor Swift Gets Seasonal." *Billboard,* December 8, 2007, Vol. 119, Issue 49, p. 89.

Kawashima, Dale. "Rising Country Star Taylor Swift Talks about Her Hit 'Tim McGraw,' Her Debut Album and Her Songwriting." *SongwriterUniverse.* c. 2005.
http://www.songwriteruniverse.com/taylorswift123.htm

"Making the Grade." *Country Weekly,* October 8, 2007, p. 10.

Neal, Chris. "Blonde Ambition." *Country Weekly,* December 3, 2007, pp. 50–52.

Saunders, Caroline. "Totally Taylor." *Justine,* December 2007/January 2008, pp. 58–67.

"A Star Is Born: Taylor Swift." *Country Weekly,* October 22, 2007, p. 52.

Swift, Taylor, as told to Kelli Acciardo. "How I Got Famous." *Seventeen,* December 2007/January 2008, p. 173.

Tarleton, Shane. "The CMAs Country Big Night." *Country Weekly,* December 3, 2007, pp. 36–37.

———. "Teen Trend-Setter." *Country Weekly,* October 8, 2007, pp. 10, 20.

"Taylor Targets Predators." *Country Weekly,* November 5, 2007, p. 58.

"The Year in Review: Country Sweeps the Country." *Cosmogirl,* December 2007/January 2008, p. 34.

On the Internet

Big Machine Records: Taylor Swift
http://www.bigmachinerecords.com/taylorswift/

Taylor Swift
www.taylorswift.com

Taylor's blog
www.myspace.com/taylorswift

INDEX